Free Verse Editions
Edited by Jon Thompson

Saint with a Peacock Voice

L. S. Klatt

Parlor Press
Anderson, South Carolina
www.parlorpress.com

Parlor Press LLC, Anderson, South Carolina, 29621

© 2025 by Parlor Press
All rights reserved.
Printed in the United States of America
S A N: 2 5 4 - 8 8 7 9

Library of Congress Cataloging-in-Publication Data on File

978-1-64317-501-0 (paperback)
978-1-64317-502-7 (pdf)
978-1-64317-503-4 (ePub)

1 2 3 4 5

Cover image: "Young Magpie Catches a Grub" by Maria Primachenko. ©1978
by the Maria Prymachenko Foundation. Used by permission.
Book design by David Blakesley.

Parlor Press, LLC is an independent publisher of scholarly and trade titles in
print and multimedia formats. This book is available in paperback and ebook
formats from Parlor Press on the World Wide Web at https://www.parlorpress.
com or through online and brick-and-mortar bookstores. For submission
information or to find out about Parlor Press publications, write to Parlor
Press, 3015 Brackenberry Drive, Anderson, South Carolina, 29621, or email
editor@parlorpress.com.

Contents

Contents

My quest, whatever it was actually for, ended with peacocks.

—Flannery O'Connor

He loved three things in life:
Evensong, white peacocks
And old maps of America

—Anna Akhmatova

Saint with a Peacock Voice

Garden Noises

Life nowadays is trash, nothing so
dirty as blood, no. The yellow moon

in the fig tree sullen, the aluminum
planets rusted. The flea only

innocent for an hour is a hitchhiker
dangerously composed, as if barely

moving but still an angel not disabled
completely, crouched with dignity

on the reddening turnip as the sun
at nightfall questions every friendless

fire in every permanent house, save
that which is painted by the peacock's voice.

Penitentiary

Good Jesus, I come to you from the green
world, a dead man ashamed. You shouldn't trust

me. I did the crime. I am a tornado
with a dreamy voice. I pray, but you ought

not to listen. You are nice people, white
teeth, pure gold. You must have recognized my

wrong before anything came out. I covered
it up, but you said I'm one of your own.

If I could paint, I would paint you a hearse,
a peanut butter automobile with bright

blue parrots under a pine tree. Truth is,
when I sing or tell a story, I see

an undertaker. I guess I'm a
disappointment. Three times I laughed at

the sunlight like I wouldn't be punished. Yes,
you are a star. I know. I shouldn't stare.

Lazy Omens, Amens

Oh whippoorwill. Gangster. Destroyer. I
cannot cope with fortune and you, her tattooed

sentinel. You cool the sun in the hazelnut tree,
leave me bareback in the changing weather.

The summer gone when I could spend the day
wrongsideout drinking Coca-Colas by

the bottle or read the prophets under the scowl
of the hills and know there was nothing too

calamitous. For the hay was new prayer;
the tractor sighed in the windy field;

and the house where I retired my body
was cheerful green timber. No future now,

whippoorwill, asking me to live every
day locked in that box, rocks in my stomach,

and listen to you eat my heart out
as the pines frazzle. I wish you were a granite

airplane that could drop out of the sky. Not
an angel, fiery and wild, screaming. Is there

kindness in your litany? What can I
salvage from the coffin where I'm hiding?

Lavender

In a world of lavender, the river
is cream. I accept this. My sudden

acceptance seems natural, God's will
even. I desire lavender, and the river

is cream. It follows that lavender
is working if life appears. It follows

strictly. The river requires desire
for compulsion. The river believes however

it believes. Life and the river reunite
in a world of lavender. It follows

strictly that lavender people are free.
I have my eye on that possibility.

The Potting Shed

I wrote about love on a Macintosh,
my Macintosh, mine. It was like writing

with a little television set. I would mouth
the words as I would see them, rouged,

and I sold them as I said them. At the end
of the line, the words engaged me

in the act then stopped. There was nothing I could
do but go somewhere else. I did.

I really tried. Except I was homesick.
The shed where I went to write was not old hat

like the Macintosh. The shed asked for
interment. Looking inside-out,

I could not slum at love. Me, a cliché,
potting my stupid wish. I meant to live.

Reluctantly

the boy who circles the yard in a blue suit
after sandwiches and Coca Colas

will feel a defect on the rose, his fingers
following the flower making contact

with bonfire, the rose as it hemorrhages.
The hook in his grasp could be called tenderness;

incurable, the hand that danced
itself raw that afternoon, the boy shocked

by the blood of his half-eaten hamburger.
Someday he will imagine fumes from the young

girl he touched in her party dress; the girl
in theory will become a city

to herself, a Long Island opened
for escapade. By the rose, she will fondle

him, his eyes bandaged. He will have fallen
lazily into her forced labor camps.

Self-Conscious

I start down the road in a Russian
automobile called the Cockroach. My ride

is humble, but I like it just fine.
It actually drives more like a mule than

an insect, my body unbearable. My heart
feels that way to me as well; I hold it

up, best I can. I can't forget the road;
the road is everything. Somewhere down the line

is Pittsburgh. I'll be sure to get there
overnight. The Cockroach needs some work,

but it's practical, better than what I used to
ride around in. I had found what I thought was

a great deal on a Formula One, fully
loaded. I would glide highfalutin by

the guilty-rich, though it didn't last. My
Russian, like my body, out of kilter

as they are, may be nothing to look at.
At the very least, they take me where I want

to go. I don't know anymore where I want
to go, and I don't like what I want.

Bodhisattva

What happened to the car? The car was
asleep. The car was absent, lost. It had

to endure. It came to accept being
a Bodhisattva, alone in the imaginary

woods, the freezing cold, where the bloodshot
fox was potentate. The car, exhausted,

waited grimly. It supposed that the purpose
of foreboding was to discover the living.

What else could the car do? It could only
give voice to the dream of the woods and the hawk

that wings slowly. It could not be aghast
at the fox going after the hawk while

the tree line caught fire. It dare not think
of the indifference of machines. None

of that was meaningful. The car returned
to the creatures, their crimson nirvana.

Light came over the car in thicknesses.
The light a dilapidated aluminum.

Wars

Probably, the deer at the ledge were afraid
of them. The fattest deer looking down,

going nowhere, reading the geraniums.
Flowers they would be glad to be chewing

but for the white. And the cold. The geraniums
white and cold below them. The deer could feel

in the throat sorry white flowers
fidgeting there. Pale flecks of geranium

that might make them sick and start them bleating
if they were to let them. Or listen to

them. Tonight, in cities, the deer will be
hunted by geraniums, uniform

white geraniums, and nobody will explain
the mechanism, how they fall into

sockets and wound the eyes, painting cities white
that were pink and brown and green and yellow;

sorry, the fat deer leaving, light-footed, going
back up the slope, the cities of

geraniums disposed. Guns blink. Houses,
complicated, fall into the river.

Crucified

the Lord crawls in traffic. Forget the company
of machines, which are rattled. Which urge

you to thrust and go around. Watch him go
away without going at all. He can move

even stopped by red light, by yellow. I love that.
With him, for the time being, I feel fast

relief. Feel friendly. Communist.
Maybe what I feel is welfare. Pheasants

are trying to sing to the crowd, and Jesus
has no objection. How could he?

Pheasants are hips and beautiful animal fat.
Their wings muscle between shoulder blades.

I wore wings once, but they didn't work. Not
very well. I didn't know where to use them. I beat

them in church and was told they were fanatics.
There are things you believe, out of time

or money, that seem uneasy for others:
the Lord is your gravy. You horn in.

Summer Fever

On 9/11, I read of beautiful
people. The beautiful have been preserved

in a mighty strange book, one about
expiation. I am looking out the window

at the last of summer, 9/11
lost on me. Catholic children sally,

come and go. Hurry, hurry, I shout
to the children. This book! It's great; it's getting

better. More novel. It's not just about
expiation but also the Fitzgeralds.

Dear children, picture victory and grace
in Minnesota. Before the pileup.

There I Go There I Hope

Milledgeville was my home; I liked Iowa,
but Milledgeville was my home. The plan was

to write anything while trusting none to see
the hospital I see. My mistake?

To please. I don't please. I am able to write
if anything will do. That said, Iowa

nurses Milledgeville, my rib
of dislike. To be hung onto. If able.

Witness

Somewhere, anywhere, nowhere God has lived.
God has lived sometimes among trees, disruptive,

and God will live even now somehow
on the downhill beneath a city whose business

is aspiration. God will level it.
Birds in gray flannel suits on Madison

Avenue, God will level them, enshrine
them. Somewhere, anywhere, nowhere a changing

light colors them. A light they multiply
like make-believe. One day they will touch the great

I am, afar in the Sahara, the light there
cunning, known for its showmanship. Birds will nest,

and without feeling one way or another
will think of God as paradise.

Thereby Paradise Thereby Hawthorne

Of the trees in the Gospels, I steer toward
the maimed, toward a wild territory

where I can lean. The trees here are such freaks,
so blunt, I tune them. Trees walking on wooden

legs. I see them as salesmen going through
a phase or criminals forgotten

in a penitentiary. Federal spirits
for a time, loosely together, on the prowl,

ready to roam if darkness will permit.
And dark it is, dark and divisive as I might

have been, tilting at trees in a bourgeois
style. I am not anti-purgatory. Anti-

is no way to heal. Anti- is a mule
without a name, a rabbit

underground. I once was an inmate here,
my mouth drastic. The Hawthorne cured me.

Charity

Speaking of parakeets, it's not untrue
they mob the sky while looking for charity

or that they listen for a tornado
in which the voice of hope is mustard-

colored. A good wind will wreck the hell
out of a city, and beyond the yellow

I can hear the taxis gasp until they
run out of time and space—I mean, Jesus,

everything in the world wants more than it can
get. Breath. Love. Whatever. There was a time

no cliché could tourniquet my windpipe;
there still are times I blow a song wide-

open over Texas; naughty, my yellow
rose that cut the tongue out of Texas.

Grand Rapids

City where snow surprised no one; where time
turned white and everything changed: snow became

snowman. Where snow hunted and killed
forgotten cars, while trees mostly hardened.

Where some stopped cold by snow walked to the liquor
store and gave up housework; where time, feeling

jittery, hesitated; where white concealed
kin, kin without houses; where the motionless

said they lived for snow then moved
to Florida. Where paperwhite became a sign

of spring and snow went on furlough; where moonlight
ran wet on the road and fish climbed a ladder.

Where I made a home in time and felt time
cheating; where snow hurt; where white hurt.

Possibly Wonderland Possibly Barcelona

Should I be afraid of myself? I shot
the hart in Montserrat, and it was no

tragedy. In fact, I was heartened. The hart
didn't accuse because it had faith.

It had great faith in the trees and woods
it discovered. There the hart could learn

without suffering, as if from the pages
of a library. The more woods, the more pages;

the more pages, the more library; on
and on. So that the woods would never want

of magic. The man kills, but the trees don't spite.
A hart is rejoicing even if the hart

is shot through. The gallstone that kills it is
plastic and the woods around it are a cathedral

great with children. On and on. Without
such a cathedral, the man who kills is

a man of earth. And the gallstone the hart
is shot with a warning about hard fact.

The Snowman

I go to my warren mildly. My mind
in the deep freeze, no light, no air. I feel

snow. I feel snow at hand. I go to my warren
mildly. The snow insolent without a rainbow.

Almost universal. But the television
is on. It thinks unobtrusively. It thinks

for itself. The television points
a .45 at my head, and grief dies

a natural death. I go to my warren
mildly. I am a child again. I horse

around with television. Paint a pathetic
picture. Force it to better everything.

Stephen Foster's Songbook Supreme

As a boy, nothing was so edifying
as My Old Kentucky Home. The affection

I have for the South I learned from my mother,
who invited me to be part of the hymn-

singing. She was energetic, so
I was not afraid in those days to

hammer my sympathy out. I know now
the song has a reputation. It is painful

to be criticized for what you were,
but this has merit, etc. Anyway,

I left my home and traveled to New
Sympathy. I am a New Yorker by desire,

of course. Millions of actors here. Some august,
some out of proportion. Actors crusade

largely for banned songs and politicians.
Nothing is nailed down, which is just as well.

My reflections on Stephen, then, are glacial
and have a good deal to do with the Church.

The Lord I Did Not Want

With a tin gun I shot God into pieces,
nothing better to do, ha ha! I was

pleased. Miracle products to keep me
thundering. Young grasshopper full of fizz

and mulberry, I always been knocked out
by the down and dark, and I had the peculiar

fortune to go off. I'm poisonous, I be
thinking when feeling like the Almighty,

pistol spitting up beautiful seed,
a thimbleful of wrath. Come one, come all,

I make a buzzard's speech in the keyhole
of the stomach. Something else I recognized

on account of my armed forces. Not easy
to click, bang, sing if you hold your breath.

The Product

I'm painting some really beautiful dogs
out in the country. They're sitting for me,

though one has arthritis. I doctor
them and give them horns. Devilish work,

painting dogs. The young one looks pleased, the mother
insulted. Both suppose they're remarkable.

The emphasis is on food, mostly. They like ducks
and chickens and sightseeing; I have to

collar them. I learned a lot about myself
last year from a painting of a cow. It

was a French one. I came insistently
all June to take the cow in. I saw it for what

it was, but I saw the painting vastly.
I learned, in French, The Cow does not

comment on politics. The painting
prefers living unaided, with buzzards.

Eastern

So the plane spilled fuel over cow country,
and I think it went to sleep. Trouble

on the plane of my devotion, which was kind
of a goodbye. A fortunate trip,

a change for the better, or so the plane
thought, hours out in the open, up in the airways,

solo, revived for a time. For a time,
it would seem to increase cordiality. If

not broken, a plane that hoped for a great
commission would be sure; it certainly

would appreciate everybody. I felt
argentine, not wary, my devotion

preserved over field and water, pilgrimage
without landing gear. Over cow country,

a little thread of fuel, a little bolt
of liquor. Spent, at rest, about to crash.

No Breath Oh Lord I Rue

Ever ready to capture God, I'm waiting
for my skin to fall off. I'm waiting to play

for the Lord inaudibly while my fingers
crack, white noise in thicket. Ten thousand fingers

as pencils drawing the imperceptible
God, leaving little tracks on an acre

of mind. That I might spit out Jerusalem
when the mind is thinking, that I might chase God

with wings and an accordion. And play
inaudibly with ten thousand friends chasing

white noise up a tree; no thought is faster
than feathers. I will be praying better

than I know how, wild bird not kicked at
or shot at, not guessed at. One name. Oh breath.

A God to Woo

I think like the worms who, overjoyed
in their unbelief, went up a ladder

to see for themselves the fire. Though it is
hardly odd to witness stars in silage

(burned-out seeds ready and waiting) the worms
had never known them to yodel or cry

the way planets do, charging red-hot overhead.
Secretly, I, too, sunrise to sunset,

eat dirt and long for flames and at night find
myself chewing the invisible edge

of moonlight. Or am I like that dog unleashed
in fields and woods, my yapping uncouth, my mouth

open to everywhere? Should a rose
burst from roadkill, would I be the first to feel

the fever? And if ever the treeless hill
is gored by lilies, how could my intention

not be to gallop away on a pink cow; call
out May day with my knife in prayer?

Lonesome

Without figs, the tree is an embarrassment;
it leaves a sweet and confusing odor,

a sooty haze. Birds will not nest in it. The tree
is restrained. Careful with its feasible

liquor. Thin. If only the fig would plum
the topmost, if only the fig would blackberry.

For praise is the root of everything.
And charity. The tree trifles with grievance;

the plague beckons. The plague beckons; the tree
shames. God fires a coal and hands it

to branches; they flare. The coal is friendly for
blackbirds who fly barbed. Querulous.

They go up and down without ladders.
Only those who quiver with the godhead

may touch fire and live. Those lonesome with knowledge
may not touch; lonesome will be cremated when figs

heap. When purple is repeated. For praise
is the root of everything. And charity.

Light Ranger

I would kill for the feeling of television.
I felt it once. I felt it holster light.

I felt it clutch me in the dark and treble
my house. All the houses. I felt the firefight

on television, the car chase, the crime
and punishment. I got caught up

in prisms, then smashed them, high on
perfume, dirty picture. Television was

blasphemy to me; it was Satan, god-
like. I wanted something heart-shaped

I hadn't had the pleasure of. My good eye glinted
languidly in a heaven without people.

Woman Painted, Refrigerated

What is it she dreams of when clumps
of snow like garbage fall, pile heavy

in a room open to silence, fall almighty
on bed and chairs, on groceries, belongings,

clumps that come quickly, come express, white
and mammoth enough to bury, lay waste,

her unthawed corpse so taut she will
not sleep or, if sleeping, put up with hail,

no hat for head, no alpaca wool
for safekeeping? Invisibility

is a power that will not voice or police,
it is snow on a stone Jesus, it is

morning in a white dress wanted by flakes
that wish to abolish the body. A

government mule will be sent to truck salt
over city street, white street, white real estate.

Winter

God drew a door. It was winter, and God
drew a door. Walked through the ice; the ice was

open, the blue suffused. God disappeared.
The frozen-skinned water parted for a woman

to become a woman, then a man. Winter
was a penitentiary where they would live.

There were animals, birds, crowds that waved.
Hyenas, wolves, bears. And monkeys. In the shale-

colored air, a linoleum owl. An owl
and a cow. God drew a door on the cow.

Several. Blue ones drawn with ice. Doors that made
noise like a harp or a forest. Doors

that were varnished. Two by two, the animals
went through forest. It was winter, no,

summer. The cow disappeared. The cow
and the hoot owl. The hoot owl was polluted.

And pink. It was fruit not fit to eat
but conditioned with pleasure. Linoleum.

God spit it out as if sour milk, then walked
on water. And the cow was everywhere.

Disenchanted Mother of Clarity

I am a woman unlikely to write.
The foggiest ideas come to me

malevolent and hopeless; I have
only the urge to strike them. The mind is

a dark enough place without me drawing
blood from it. But let's suppose that there is

a spotlight waiting within the heart,
and the heart is innocent because it is

made of paper and can be cut, and the hurt
is good health. A cut would give me reason

to type. I could put my finger in the hurt;
I might like the pressure. What would come

of a paper heart made raw by the spotlight?
Or a plaster head left out in red rain?

River with Cancer and Sorrow

River? I'm rid of the river. Time
ran out on the shriveled, cold stream.

I walk barefoot, baptized in sassafras,
afflicted by treetops and singing a

high note to paradise. I lay my eyes
on the ginger-colored empire, my tongue

a violent butterfly, something strange and gold.
If that's what faith is, I'll say it's enough,

I'll say I'll never want, I'll sleep serene
in the clear morning sun. I have a direction.

I'm looking for fortune. Eyes waste nothing;
ears listen to honeysuckle for thirteen

years. Shaking one foot then another, I move
my exaggerated skeleton. I favor

a gasping hymn and get into wild trouble.
I count no more the distance from sick

to unclean. Go on, I say, you are
somebody. You have tiptoed somewhere real.

This Haloed Earth

My sullen mind ails me. Inauspicious
thoughts parade above the crepe-myrtle

and flutter carefully where the mowing
machine cannot get at them. The galaxy

at night, restless. Recurrent. Let planets
crash; let peacocks flock. Like a sullen king

I will bronze what I see with un-
favorable suns. But moths in the garden

range quietly as long as daylight
contends—moths dusk sent to underwrite

flowers, awaken birds, bantams. Moths,
with Cleopatra wings folded, invisible

to the universe. Amen. My dreams
multiply, uncontrolled. They go

where they go. The majority mild
as chrysanthemums. Not denouncing.

Salute to the Union in Light of John Wesley

The Girl Scout at war with the Boy Scout went
to kiss the gladiola of his heart,

but the heart was more machine than corsage,
though in a deeper place it opened.

The heart was happy to have cheated death
by murmuring the way grass might have

had it been spring. The war had to do with
a feeling that there was a beautiful quiver

between them, a glass bow which if she broke
would cause his knees to buckle. The quiver

was clear as a bell, and the music it made
was decent and sweet. But they looked at it

critically as children desperate
to police it. It was probably the moon-

shaped sword that held Girl and Boy at attention,
and the questions of when and how to use

the bow, beautiful as it was, rigid as it was,
ready to play at night for anxious stars.

Boy

I got a bone to pick with angels, the knife
and fork they take from me. They jump when no one

is after them; scream wildcat if I go nosing;
judge me, but I won't stay put. I hum their names

like I do the rabbit; fire their wails
as I climb high in the woods. I got pain

same as them; never let body and blood hush
me. Fall over backwards and bolt upright

to wait on the Lord. Cow in the hollow,
I got her. Bat in the house, I eased it

out gentle. I feel called to the animal.
Whatever I kill, I remember. Kill

it good, if I have to. No waving or gasping
for reason, since what I say is golden.

The muscles of my throat jerk nothing
softly; I hear angels muttering.

Business as Usual

The toolshed back of the house was where, running
from family disputes and rough language,

I would strum a child's guitar, a joke of a thing.
It made me laugh to sing-song in the shack and, quick

out the door, gabble with birds in the mulberry
tree and voice my pleasure until one day

the guitar went haywire. Everybody
I knew was looking to make their way

in the world, their first million, but soon enough
any money in hand would blow up (hand-

grenade) and the easy life they hoped for would be
desecrated. Not so strange those days to spot

at the edge of the field a man named Backbone,
a shadow of himself since going bankrupt

but an intruder just the same, thieving
everything of little significance

on our farm—nails, harrow, a spent fuse, brake
line, the odd wheel rim, rusty drive train.

With a wagon, he would drag the heap
to his yard. Week to week, Backbone picked out

pieces he admired from the pile to repair,
that is, he would machine the daylight

out of them. The man had vision, for sure,
but welcome him? We did not. Resented

how he fondled the tractor parts with which
we alone were familiar and on which

we planned our triumph. Though left behind,
the mess was our obligation, not his.

Elvis Minor

Sometimes I feel, believable as I am,
I am only an amateur. Elvis

in body but not in mind. And not
even body since the artist known as Elvis

is ever-changing, grotesque. For one to be
seen, one has to be looked at. Perverse

to ask if I am really there. Does Elvis
ask this? In a way, Elvis invented

himself, at least, his disciples say so. The fiction
is Gothic, Southern through and through.

I may know the South, but that doesn't make me Elvis
or give me the gist of him. Kind of a shock

to suffer as an artist. I thought I would
devour the audience, live grandly and slick.

Yet I shift in and out of my body
advertising myself, diseased. Look at me

fading, poor, poor in spirit, lest you believe
America is true and/or classless.

Lamblike

I chase the buffalo; I chase it
anywhere. I chase it all the way to New

Buffalo. There is a chance the chase will last
for years and years. New Buffalo seems

phony. Like an unctuous myth, it plagues
the mind. However, to most, the new

is favorable. Not for long, though. I suppose
I am Catholic about old buffalo,

buffalo prime. You don't get over your first,
even if, for now, it is going

away. I see it immolating. Like
an opera. I love the opera

of the buffalo. I am about to
unveil it. It is called eulogy when you

care for something wonderful, something that
has saved you. True, all true. But what if as you care

you tame? That seems akin to religion,
not revival. Buck it, I guess. Lamblike.

However

I am snow without direction; havoc
ensues when I essay. How can I face

the world snow destroys after I blow it,
measure who I am, right violence? For whom

is snow innocent? A comfort my death
with the help of metamorphoses. I melt.

Get lighter. Preserve the lime twig, devoted
to what it needs. My issue is doubtless,

and together snow and I will be
respectful, if also unpredictable.

Umbrella

What can be done with an old man in a raincoat?
Undress him? Make him wear a paper

garment? Okay, but that may not work. Undress
him again and put him in another

coat, an iron one? What if he growls? Box up
all his clothes then; he might be happier

denuded. Right. Let him go natural
in his ape suit, sensitive to storm

and light. A surprise to himself
advertising nothing but his person,

free to dart, building to building, moonlit
in a downpour of kindness. There would be few,

like him, torpedoed. Few with virtue
and courage. Few as open as him, half up,

half down. An umbrella for other
people: the just, the not just. One could fashion

a better city with a lifelike (life-size)
gorilla. Name it Human. Or something.

The Last Librarian

Years ago, a man felt America
tempting him. America, what a god,

great body. The man was not suspicious
of all the praise the god obliged. I say

America; it might have been Ireland
or Russia. Perhaps art, and not a country

at all. But if art, it was an unusual
art, one that also infected. Given

what it was, the man sinned constantly.
In this wonderful country, years ago,

a man with no head for business felt
rather grand and spiritual, his encounter

with art religious, to the point of being
unending. Apologetic, as well.

That was its demise. The man would have a hard
time with demise. Art dead

now had to be mystical. To cope, the man
started writing a book, an antidote for what

he felt and why. The book was a diary
of a country. Readable. I am reading

it now, and I have to say I countenance
this America. More than that, I believe

in it as a Protestant. I cannot do
otherwise, so close I am to eclipse.

Doomsday a New Day

Listen, Doomsday. You can't clean the White House
talking trash. Or a white church with dirty

money. There's no sunburst in that. If you want
more than a heap, you need a bucket

of blood and battalions of Lincolns. Eyes
upon eyes that see the color of

everything. The red fern, the blue dream, the brown
Jesus, even the gold calf. How is it,

Doomsday, that white washes the hands
of hurts? What god signs off on that? As a boy,

you glided over the earth and through a door
like a bear on a bicycle. The earth

was glass, the bear invisible, and the door
did not appreciate anything

that was unintelligible. But there
you went, buttering the road with unnatural

light. Dream light. The light of the world
made you feel lavender inside you.

My Kinsman General Washington

I was friends with a narrow fellow in the grass,
lethal at the bone. He was my good-

natured cousin George. The things he said,
he said plainly. George was real vanilla.

Time has proved his words (their complexion)
could be poisonous. Victims died

for the sake of Washington, picturesque
hero on a hill, raucous and appalling.

They ran through fields and woods for him, and he
for them. Since he's been gone, I've looked

to the sky. I've searched Zarathustra
for a liberating star, the wild Christ

child. And asked for barred owls. A better
country. Where citizens don't disappear.

Or the tree toad. The truth about my greenhouse:
azaleas will rebel there, black out.

Toward a Deeper Pretending

The solid fact of the battleship
must once in a while destroy the dull gaze

of the material world and bring itself
roundabout to stop under a cloudless sky

while losing its heavy attitude; must know
that, obscene as it is, the point

of the battleship is to believe that
consciousness is a godsend in the mind's

weather, the joy of it beyond phantasm,
even though the brain wants to be detached

and not aware of incurable tears
that hurt the eyes (they are so

spiritual) and outrage those who are light
sensitive. Remorse is sometimes ugly

like the battleship, contemptuous, taking
up arms rather than surrendering

to green, blue, and purple waves, such as those
of the peacock, who, when fanning his

philosophical tail as an afterthought
or insinuation, is real enough.

Nose, Mustache, and Spectacles

The disappearing icebergs are glad,
happy to shadow the artificial man,

his impudent face grinning, as if not
understanding how to look at the white

hot city, the exasperated desert
where water, gliding insistently, is

indispensable, like sapphire, if only
the icebergs could be endless. That black ice,

too, might be a spigot, blessing (by boom
and moonlight glistening) the dark interval,

the artificial man will not discover.
His head is full of chemical hush. Paradise

and despair (which one guides?) go before him
on the keen smell of sardines, while to say

that cockroaches jaw, light-years away, is
a sudden but reasonable depravity.

Dreams and Other Inconveniences

In dreams, combat. My mind is weak in dreams,
minor. Or sometimes a millstone will hold it

down while an ax is wielded. Dreams only
a cardinal will transmit by means of

radiance. I want a cardinal for the labor
of this day. And radiance. I can be

violent about it, but violence doesn't
embody anything. Any more than fiat

or personality. Dreams come
when they come. If they do. A cardinal

is a total waste, which is why I wolf
it down. The dogma of dreams glorifies

excess. My wolf lives in peril at the outermost
darkness where light is ultimate.

Red Weather

I don't live far from a lake of fire, a lake
so clear I can view my own likeness.

I climb barefoot down the embankment
and see in my reflection neither saint

nor angel but a white elephant, dead in
the water, triumphant in failure.

I deign never to close my eyes, though what
I want is unintelligible to the must

of the crotch, the whip of the tail. Nor do
I refuse to look for heaven in my stomach,

which has spent a fortune gorging on hornets
hostile to the mind. The trunks of my legs

churn; body and blood swim absently
against the undertow. I will reach the clouds

not because there is something electric
about hornets but because the blue

mouth in its disposition will talk helplessly
and homesick with every stroke.

Anywhere under the Sky

there's a lonesome harmonica. The music
it monkeys with smells like God's lips.

The rabbits in the garden are sentenced
by the song, as well as a violet note

that astonishes them. The rabbits dilate
periwinkle eyes. They know enough about

how hard times are to freak out. They
are almost eaten up by the crazy

harmonica, but, while a Ghost always
is present (above, below, and all around),

it desecrates not the garden, it desecrates
not the pasture. Blooms of praise

are lost in the rabbit heads, hymns to watermelon
and sugar cane and the blue ox on the farm.

The rabbits are saved by the mercy
of the mouth organ since neither guitar

nor piano watch out for blood, nor do
they catch the purple sass of martyrdom

in a pig's tail. The harmonica
is played blow by blow, as if laughing.

Astronaut

Let's talk about what happened; how we each
put on an earth suit; the way we launched

our bones carelessly, sang out to a night
loud with stars, ate cake. Both of us, fanatic,

reached for the random animal, frog
as well as rat. We liked that rat. Jumped

out of our skin, threw the baseball with
impunity. Pitched it up to God in disbelief,

solidarity. Astronaut, tell me
how, years later, we would be severed—

me missing hands and nerves as I explain
myself to the universe. You leaving

in a spaceship drugged with ketchup
and artificial orange. You, who were so

attached to our penitentiary,
smile gingerly at fugitive speed. Gone.

The Good to Come

We consent to a sea-change, Lincoln shot,
the shot glances off; we picture him safe

once more in Eden, anything possible.
Fiction pleases. The good (the best)

has not yet left the world. Reverse that. The world
is too much with him. Lincoln going on

and on for ages. Which seems sort of familiar,
textbook even, like algebra or history.

In the movies, the past is often held up.
The situation raises our hackles,

and yet.... On behalf of all of us, there is
something subtler (more human) to come than

Lincoln haphazard. Something evolutionary,
innate. Whether American or not.

Medusa

It may be that religion tries to purify
the supernatural. That piety

is scandalized by sex and the obscene.
One could make the case that Medusa

is gone. There is no other if the other
is stone. Or worse, if the other

is dearth. And what if the mysteries
become blind, impregnable? Who would see

God for who she is? I am afraid of her,
her creative body and field of vision.

Widespread

This sentence may run off like the giraffe
on the tablecloth I'm folding. The folding

creates movement. As does time. A writer
is seldom free enough to play

with a giraffe, put it into missionary
position. Animal rights won't let that

happen. But something has to happen,
something massive. A careless sentence will plunge

a giraffe into a river. The creative
must tend to it. To tend does not mean killing

the animal. Somewhat arbitrarily,
a patrolman several years away at a zoo

might feel violent. There, timepiece in hand,
the patrolman would be told to set up

roadblocks, but in the dark, his mind open
to anything, a baboon could be woven

into the sequence. If so, the imagination
might damage itself, clarifying.

Clarifying rather than folding.
When something like compassion or truthfulness

is needed, I'm happy enough folding
a tablecloth, the movement of it.

Short Letter from Exile

I doubt I have the right to be this cheerful.
I'm in too sorry a shape to send myself

anywhere on a shoestring. I would like to be
shot out like Armstrong so I can't be

forgotten. But forgotten I am, without
portrait, self-portrait. I didn't put

something in Tennessee. What I thought
was novel some called spare on reflection.

Unfortunately tied to myself, my exile
didn't please. I guess they are wise to my accent.

I still play with colors, copy nice. However,
a good word is holding me up.

Admonishment

The footnote went into the desert; how
could it face the mob? The god in it

neither man nor woman but hermitic
the way a St. might be. The footnote came

across as carrot-colored, effeminate.
It arrived, a philosopher gazing at

Badlands. The Badlands mattered; they stayed with
the footnote for days. There was rage, but love

would conquer it. Is that what I meant, that love
would conquer ruin, a book of tears for

desert? Read the gray of St. Footnote,
the carrot-colored conviction. It put

eyes on the artist who was everywhere not
an accident. In the book of life. At work.

Strangers Maybe Saints

We are weak, not ignorant. We are guided
by a weak and happy sun, and in our boats

we thunder with unveiled mind. Serene boats
request peaceful separations. A land

beyond province and sorrows. Lonely
and at home in a child's country, we gaze

at the feet, not the face, of God. We glory
in separations, movements of light

for the weak and happy. The sun
on our boats serene, maybe crushed. We joy;

we thunder. With a life whose unveiled light
lies beyond mind. And God is always.

Wantonness

I love snapdragons. I am ecstatic
about snapdragons intermingled. Once in

a while, though, you need the rain to clear
the paragraph you write of profusion.

I am ready to love the rain, even the rain
that has plinked colorful hats when I have taken

the typewriter fishing. In the creek there,
in the cold water, I am a catcher.

The distressed are jumping and jerking, thinking
about biting, also being swallowed

by the believable. I am a believer
myself in the rain and in the things I type,

though the weather is ready to kill off
too many, the sickly, yes, but also

the inane and displeasing. It's cloudy
this morning, but I am not grayer,

am I, sitting listlessly? I feel ripe.
I get one sentence out then another.

Automatic, this snapdragon profusion.
Then something new like a hookworm.

Violets

As violets in the gateway bloom, the valiant
light ceases. The so-called light. One

feels it in the ground underfoot. But for
the ground, the rabbit will rebel. Rabbit

going up to a light extreme. The going
is voluntary, a blessing. The violets

do not foster war; they doubt it. With one
exception. A bloom that roots for peril.

It belongs to the others but exists
apart. It is not the light, but a property

of it. And of clay. Light and clay.
The others gasping for purer air are

only delighted. They color the world
same as the white, while the bloom that roots for

peril seems grim. In moral danger.
Bent in the gateway, it is valiant.

Pristine

I had to read The Scarlet Elephant
in school. Did you? I couldn't avoid it.

My teacher said it was the bedrock
of American literature. She said

the author was afraid of God and other
raw forces. A good deal of psychology

went into it, which I like, though I
didn't actually get through the book. Way

too many words. Too much history.
I think the elephant was kind of vain,

and the blind man who had to kill it was
a piece of work, the least common

denominator. The blind man handled
the elephant like a bomb. That it was scarlet

deviled him because he couldn't see
it but was certain it had to be there.

My teacher said whenever anything
put on scarlet you knew that was primary.

It still freaks me out the time she set fire to
The Elephant and viewed the act as piety.

The Kingdom of Vigor

Children, the kingdom of vigor
is unlike a cat on the lookout for

a crow-filled tree; when facing it, the cat
resists going up it. Or the kingdom

of vigor is unlike the crow-filled seed;
though time to grow, it offers complaints

because something imperceptible has laid
hold of it. I say to you, children,

the kingdom of vigor is unlike even
a frog dissected to the point

of being violent, and the soul, feeling
dissected itself, becomes invisible.

I'm talking myself true; such a kingdom
of bodies is unlikely. Go and find it

in the allegory. Then sing like
the convict you are beyond enlightenment.

Visible

The hyenas glanced casually at the pig
in the meadow, not interested enough

to drag it away. Before, they had laughed
at the pig, howled at it. They were in a lather,

then they weren't. Sanely, the hyenas this day
elected to blunt their reasoning; not

actually campaign for the razorback;
not actually tamper with it. The new

rules were jarring; they forgot they were
hyenas. Not quite. One snickered

at the pig and expected to corner
it. But the pig approached absently,

possibly in cool tones, so that it changed
its tune. Hyenas without heat, hyenas

confused. In the time it took to dismiss
the clear path, the path glared and everything

in the meadow flushed, yes sir. The sun
when it stopped for the night hoarsely grunted.

Red Letter Elvis

Elvis does not promise meaning, never
did. His dancers are impressionistic

like a horse, half in, half out of Chicago,
and a policeman makes a run for it.

I hate the thought of forgetting the horse,
the whole business of the horse, but the meaning

won't keep. Not the half of it. Out or in.
I find in Elvis the story is on

the surface, real. You don't have to impose
it. Or you do, but it's like babel, your feelings.

You dynamite the feelings if the babel
doesn't shut up. If the feelings read frantic.

America was a quandary for Presley,
an experiment. Theologically,

Elvis had to defeat the lack of meaning
in America in order for America

to discover him. The sound of defeat
he condensed. The sound hurt law and order,

the business of '56. It did not
escape the Great Fire or slide by.

Because of Said Thrash in My Loins

I gave my heart to said panther. How quickly
it found my abdomen. Pulled out my liver

instead of being satisfied with the agreed
upon pound of flesh. Went for my head

as well and took what was there, the unease
I call my own. The panther dragged last sign

of me through honeysuckle and
garden. I saw but did not understand

the fly who approached. Heard but did not grasp
the byzantine language. It was first to speak;

then came a tiger dressed in the flowers
of the Buddha and an owl

on a wing of saffron. The United States
of beasts pinned my hands and feet, and I remembered

certain foreign parts of me, such as
the apple stuck in my throat where the worm

would arabesque. I paid for the kiss of Christ
as he chewed the apple, leaving welts

I could not acknowledge without cursing
the earth, which meant selling the garden.

Like Other Desperate Animals

I celebrate my conversion to a cosmic
life. I travail but happily.

I place a jar in Tennessee. Absurd,
I feel love in my language bones.

The bones come along and apace. With bias.
They come along with bread in their jar. I place

the jar in Tennessee, the heart of it.
Word is the bread is broken. You can taste

Camus in it. Sometimes Augustine.
A bedrock increasingly broken for you,

and with great force. To gloss a universe,
I jar the anguish. Nothing is vanity.

Invocation

Loving this book may be immediate.
You may feel a leap in you that will point

to the mystical. You need love; this book
is drowning in experience. The bishop

is fighting the current, which is for you
a choice. You choose it. You inherited pain,

neglect, but you need the bishop; you may collapse.
The bishop is where? In the asking. You

remember everything fit to say; the bishop
wins when you search for interpretation.

What is the point, then, if the book loses
the authority to love you, hope for you?

Note on the Composition

This collection is made of 100% recycled material culled from the collected works of Flannery O'Connor (minus the two novels). Each poem harvests language exclusively from a particular O'Connor story, essay, or letter, and recasts a subset of these words (unaltered for tense, number, or grammar) into lyric expression, specifically couplets. The exceptions to this constraint are the occasional fusing of single words into double words (e.g., "green" + "house" = "greenhouse"), a liberty to capitalize or not capitalize words as I see fit, the infrequent updating of O'Connor's spellings to reflect current standards, the intentional modification of "McIntosh" to "Macintosh" in "The Potting Shed," and the abbreviation of a date (from "9/11/52" to "9/11") in "Summer Fever."

These poems are not intended to restate what O'Connor has delivered already so potently in dramatic or expository form but to explore what else her diction, in the mouth of another, might want to say. The poems, then, are not erasures or paraphrases; rather, they recycle and rearrange selected words available in the texts. My intention has not been to disrespect or loot O'Connor's oeuvre like some tomb raider. The opposite is true. By composing poems in her register, I hope to deepen my readers' experience with the texture of her material while also demonstrating that language is a renewable resource. The words O'Connor uses—all of us use—can be replanted in new genres, new gardens. Thus, in this project, I celebrate the resilience of words, in this case, those words that appear to be spoken for (used up) and therefore taken out of circulation but which, in fact, are still fecund.

The poems in this project were composed well before the ascent of AI and do not rely on algorithms. For better or worse, each arrangement of O'Connor's language is custom-made by my own brain.

Acknowledgments

The author gratefully acknowledges the following publications in which poems from the manuscript first appeared. "A God to Woo" and "Business as Usual" in *The Southern Review*, "Penitentiary" and "Lazy Omens, Amens" in *Carolina Quarterly*, "Disenchanted Mother of Clarity" in *Image*, "Winter" in *Seneca Review*, "Grand Rapids" in *Crazyhorse*, "The Product" in *DIAGRAM*, "Bodhisattva" in *32 Poems*, "River with Cancer and Sorrow" in *Juxtaprose*, "Light Ranger" in *The Common*, "However" in *The Encounter: A Handbook of Poetic Practice*, "Garden Noises" and "The Lord I Did Not Want" in *Kenyon Review* (*KR Online*).

The author also expresses gratitude for a sabbatical from Calvin University and a residency at The Hermitage Artist Retreat, where several of these poems were composed. Special thanks to Jon Thompson, editor of Free Verse Editions, and David Blakesley, founder and publisher of Parlor Press, for their skillful effort in putting this volume together.

Poems and Sources

The poems in this volume sample language from Flannery O'Connor's collected prose and remix it, one poem per work. Her sentences, her narratives, her arguments have been dissolved and reconstituted into couplets, into a new order entirely. This vocabulary of hers, celebrated and ardently rearranged, expresses my own original thoughts, sentiments, and imagination. Readers interested in which of my poems correspond to the O'Connor prose pieces may consult the following table:

Poem	O'Connor Story
Penitentiary	A Good Man Is Hard To Find
Garden Noises	The Life You Save May Be Your Own
River With Cancer and Sorrow	The River
The Lord I Did Not Want	A Stroke of Good Fortune
Anywhere under The Sky	A Temple of the Holy Ghost
Nose, Mustache, and Spectacles	The Artificial Nigger
Lazy Omens, Amens	A Circle of Fire
Salute to The Union in Light of John Wesley	A Late Encounter with the Enemy
Toward a Deeper Pretending	Good Country People
Business as Usual	The Displaced Person
Disenchanted Mother of Clarity	Everything that Rises Must Converge
A God to Woo	Greenleaf
Red Weather	A View of the Woods
Bodhisattva	The Enduring Chill
Charity	The Comforts of Home
Astronaut	The Lame Shall Enter First
Doomsday a New Day	Revelation
Because of Said Thrash in My Loins	Parker's Back
Woman Painted, Refrigerated	Judgment Day
Wars	The Geranium
Visible	The Barber
Boy	Wildcat

Wantonness	The Crop
No Breath Oh Lord I Rue	The Turkey (minus The Capture)
Grand Rapids	The Train
Admonishment	Why Do the Heathen Rage?
My Kinsman General Washington	The Partridge Festival
Light Ranger	An Afternoon in the Woods
Umbrella	Enoch and the Gorilla
Crucified	The Peeler
Winter	The Heart of the Park
Lonesome	You Can't Be Any Poorer Than Dead
Poem	**O'Connor Essay**
Elvis Minor	The Fiction Writer and His Country
Violets	The Regional Writer
This Haloed Earth	The King of the Birds
Medusa	The Church and the Fiction Writer
Thereby Paradise Thereby Hawthorne	Some Aspects of the Grotesque in Southern Fiction
Reluctantly	Introduction to a Memoir of Mary Ann
The Good to Come	Fiction Is a Subject with a History—It Should Be Taught That Way
Witness	The Catholic Novelist in the Protestant South
Widespread	The Nature and Aim of Fiction
Self-Conscious	Writing Short Stories
The Kingdom of Vigor	On Her Own Work (Hollins College)
Lavender	On Her Own Work (Letters to McCarthy)
Pristine	The Teaching of Literature
Like Other Desperate Animals	Novelist and Believer
Dreams and Other Inconveniences	Catholic Novelists and Their Readers
Poem	**O'Connor Letter (Library of America)**
There I Go There I Hope	To E. Hardwick & R. Lowell [886]
The Product	To Robert Lowell [896]

Summer Fever	To Caroline Gordon Tate [899]
Stephen Foster's Songbook Supreme	To Erik Langkjaer [936]
The Snowman	To Ben Griffith [937]
Lamblike	To Elizabeth Bishop [1126]
However	To John Hawkes [1146]
Poem	**O'Connor Letter (*The Habit of Being*)**
Strangers, Maybe Saints	To Janet McKane [592]
Possibly Wonderland Possibly Barcelona	To A. [287]
The Potting Shed	To Maryat Lee [203]
The Last Librarian	To Dr. T. R. Spivey [303]
Invocation	To Alfred Corn [484]
Eastern	To Sally & Robert Fitzgerald [281]
Short Letter from Exile	To Elizabeth McKee [88]
Red Letter Elvis	To A. [186]

About the Author

L. S. Klatt's poetry has appeared in various magazines and anthologies, including *Harvard Review, Denver Quarterly, Crazyhorse, Copper Nickel, Poetry Daily, The Believer, Best American Poetry, Image, The Common, The Southern Review,* and *The New Yorker.* His first book, *Interloper,* won the Juniper Prize, awarded by the University of Massachusetts Press. His second, *Cloud of Ink,* garnered the Iowa Poetry Prize from the University of Iowa Press. He also has published essays on poets, most recently "Kenneth Koch, Cincinnatian, Poet of Confetti" in *The Cincinnati Review* and "Blue Buzz, Blue Guitar: Wallace Stevens and the Poetics of Noisemaking" in *The Georgia Review.* Klatt lives and works in Grand Rapids, Michigan, where he formerly served as poet laureate of the city.

Photograph of L. S. Klatt.

Free Verse Editions

Edited by Jon Thompson

13 ways of happily by Emily Carr
& in Open, Marvel by Felicia Zamora
& there's you still thrill hour of the world to love by Aby Kaupang
Alias by Eric Pankey
the atmosphere is not a perfume it is odorless by Matthew Cooperman
At Your Feet (A Teus Pés) by Ana Cristina César, edited by
    Katrina Dodson, trans. by Brenda Hillman and Helen Hillman
Bari's Love Song by Kang Eun-Gyo, translated by Chung Eun-Gwi
Between the Twilight and the Sky by Jennie Neighbors
Blade Work by Lily Brown
Blood Orbits by Ger Killeen
The Bodies by Christopher Sindt
The Book of Isaac by Aidan Semmens
The Calling by Bruce Bond
Canticle of the Night Path by Jennifer Atkinson
Child in the Road by Cindy Savett
Civil Twilight by Giles Goodland
Condominium of the Flesh by Valerio Magrelli, trans. by Clarissa Botsford
Contrapuntal by Christopher Kondrich
Country Album by James Capozzi
Cry Baby Mystic by Daniel Tiffany
The Curiosities by Brittany Perham
Current by Lisa Fishman
Day In, Day Out by Simon Smith
Dear Reader by Bruce Bond
Dismantling the Angel by Eric Pankey
Divination Machine by F. Daniel Rzicznek
Elsewhere, That Small by Monica Berlin
Empire by Tracy Zeman
Erros by Morgan Lucas Schuldt
Extinction of the Holy City by Bronisław Maj, trans. by Daniel Bourne
Fifteen Seconds without Sorrow by Shim Bo-Seon, trans. by
    Chung Eun-Gwi and Brother Anthony of Taizé
The Forever Notes by Ethel Rackin
The Flying House by Dawn-Michelle Baude
General Release from the Beginning of the World by Donna Spruijt-Metz
Ghost Letters by Baba Badji

A Suit of Paper Feathers by Nate Duke
Summoned by Guillevic, trans. by Monique Chefdor & Stella Harvey
Sunshine Wound by L. S. Klatt
System and Population by Christopher Sindt
There Are as Many Songs in the World as Branches of Coral by
    Elizabeth Jacobson
These Beautiful Limits by Thomas Lisk
They Who Saw the Deep by Geraldine Monk
The Thinking Eye by Jennifer Atkinson
This History That Just Happened by Hannah Craig
An Unchanging Blue: Selected Poems 1962–1975 by
    Rolf Dieter Brinkmann, trans. by Mark Terrill
Under the Quick by Molly Bendall
Verge by Morgan Lucas Schuldt
The Visible Woman by Allison Funk
The Wash by Adam Clay
Well by Sasha Steensen
We'll See by Georges Godeau, trans. by Kathleen McGookey
What Stillness Illuminated by Yermiyahu Ahron Taub
Winter Journey [Viaggio d'inverno] by Attilio Bertolucci, trans. by
    Nicholas Benson
Wonder Rooms by Allison Funk